ONCE UPON A DREAM

South West Verses

Edited By Donna Samworth

First published in Great Britain in 2017 by:

Young Writers Est. 1991

Young Writers
Remus House
Coltsfoot Drive
Peterborough
PE2 9BF
Telephone: 01733 890066
Website: www.youngwriters.co.uk

FOREWORD

Welcome to 'Once Upon a Dream – South West Verses'.

For our 'Once Upon A Dream' competition, we invited primary school pupils to delve within their deepest imaginations and create poetry inspired by dreams. They were not limited to the dreams they experience during their sleep, they were free to explore and describe their dreams and aspirations for the future, what could inspire a dream, and also the darker side of dreams... the nightmare!

The topic proved to be hugely popular, with children dreaming up the cleverest, craziest and, sometimes, creepiest of poems! The entries we received showcase the writing talent and inspired imaginations of today's budding young writers.

Congratulations to Harry Corber, who has been selected as the best poet in this anthology, hopefully this is a dream come true! Also a big well done to everyone whose work is included within these pages, I hope seeing it published help you continue living your writing dreams!

Donna Samworth

CONTENTS

Chloe Ann West (8)	65
Lois Hodge (9)	66
Danny Mike Parkinson (9)	67
Jade Joy (8)	68
Evie Fay Baker (9)	69
Laura Devine (9)	70
Eliza Burt (9)	71
Sadie Faye Roach (8)	72
Abigail Carter (9)	73
Yousef Akka (9)	74
Oliver Bowditch (9)	75
Kalia Topaz Bracey (9)	76
Xan Staal (8)	77
Joshua Paul Harper (9)	78
Abigail Record (8)	79
Lily Stantiford (9)	80
Salma Akka (9)	81
Gala Nickels (9)	82
Jamie Oldershaw (9)	83
Ryan Burt (9)	84
Fred Battersby (9)	85
Perry Allen (9)	86
Lily Mann (8)	87
Harry James Hawker (9)	88
Summer Jorja Parsons (9)	89

Brockworth Primary Academy, Brockworth

Jamol Dare (12)	90
Jaquan Carmica Smith (11)	91
Filip Mihalik (11)	92
Casey Thomas (11)	93
Amelie Witts (11)	94
Adrian Midlane (11)	95
Lacey Ann Richardson (11)	96

Deane Discovery Centre, Blagdon Hill

Edward Patrick Harry Parsons (10)	97
Wraith Haysom (11)	98
Charlie Teasdale (8)	99

Travis Norman (10)	100
Ty Chick (9)	101

Ford Primary School, Ford

Alisha Jannette Davies (8)	102
Jensen Harrison (9)	103
Christian Webber (9)	104
Jessica Lee (9)	105
Tazmin Hopkins (9)	106
McKenzie James Bird (8)	107
Amy May Parmenter (8)	108
Isabelle Jayne Hutton (9)	109
Kobi Collins (9)	110

Halberton Primary School, Halberton

Sophie Artis (9)	111
Poppy Sharland (10)	112
Freya May Davis (10)	114
Harry Lejeune (9)	115
Meisha Clapp (10)	116
Rupert Awcock (9)	117
Alicia Sugden (9)	118
James Elliott (9)	119
Millie Crane (9)	120
Eden Jones (9)	121
Lola Hughes (9)	122

Milton Park Primary School, Weston-Super-Mare

Kacy Lucas (8)	123
Patryk Gabriel Zapotoczny (9)	124
James Horlick (9)	125
George Richard Hartley (9)	126
Finlay Francis-Carter (9)	127
Alicia Bessant (8)	128
Harry Tedder (9)	129
Charlotte Louise Cooper (8)	130
Ruby Edwards (9)	131
Jack Ford (9)	132
Jacob Alexander Mogg (9)	133

Ellie Marie Havard (9) 134
Laura Widzisz (9) 135
Reuben Harding-Blake (8) 136
Alyssa Edwards (9) 137
Aston White (9) 138
Kayleigh Turnbull (8) 139

Oasis Academy New Oak, Hengrove

Callum Cairns (9) 140
Chelsea Ince (9) 142
Courtney Kizza (9) 143
Hamza Sorgucu (10) 144
Ava Bendall (10) 145
Thomas Culverhouse (10) 146
Liam Ferris (10) 147
Kian Gwilliam (10) 148
Megan Paige Williams (10) 149
Laya-Aria Gharyal (10) 150
Charlotte Elizabeth Collins (10) 151

Shakespeare Primary School, Honicknowle

Malakai Parsons (10) 152
Harry Marshall Hoskin (9) 153
James Michael Hacker (10) 154
Tyler Reid (10) 155
Radu Stefan Munteanu (10) 156
Lewis Bennett (10) 157
Kelisa Moate (10) 158

Stoke Fleming Community Primary School, Stoke Fleming

India Darburn (11) 159
Alfie Rogers (9) 160
Rosie Dorothy Coombes 161
Allen (11)
Iona McGhee (11) 162
Frankie Baker (11) 163
Ethan Prettyjohns (10) 164
Kieran Wells (11) 165

Weston All Saints Primary School, Weston

Lydia Shearman (9) 166
Rhiannon Williams (9) 168
Olive Matilda Hosker (9) 169
Jaylen G-S (9) 170
Daniel Lawrence (9) 171
Jack C (8) 172
Annabelle Hicks (9) 173
William Michael H (9) 174
Sara Gabriela Stoica (9) 175

Yeo Valley Primary School, Barnstaple

Andrew Dyer (10) 176
Lily Rose Morton (9) 177
Keila Beales-Neill (9) 178
Leo Luxton (11) 179
Ella Westwood (10) 180
Liam Leslie (10) 181

THE POEMS

Well done! Your poem has been chosen as the best in this book.

My Imagination

I n my imagination, I could see a green, hungry dinosaur

M y heart jumped when I heard him roar,

A s soon as I saw him, my heart started to rapidly beat

G oing as fast as I could, I fell to my feet

I turned around and couldn't believe my eyes

N ext to the dinosaur was a great human pie

A gain, I started to run, as fast as I could go

T hen it fell silent but there's one thing you should know

I n my imagination, he turned into a crow

O verhead it flew above the buildings and streams

N ext time you see a dinosaur, it may not be what it seems.

Harry Corber (10)
Shakespeare Primary School, Honicknowle

Animals

Animals are great
Animals are fun
They play all day in the sun.
Once I saw one on the street
It looked like it needed something to eat.
So I gave it leftovers from my tea
And then it said, 'Yippee, Yippee!'
Then next day I saw it in the pet shop.
I said, 'Mum can I buy that dog in the pet shop?'
She said, 'Yes, It's called Pop'
So I bought it, it was ten pounds.
All the animals were cute, I looked all around.
When we went out, it was freezing cold
Even Pop's feet were as cold as ice
And one man was bald.
When we got home she jumped up.
Bash went the glass!
Crash went the vase!

Iona Hambly (8)
All Saints East Clevedon CE Primary, Clevedon

Joe Land

A land of dreams that nobody hates
A land of everything you could want
Pizza, sausages, get them here
Plus we have the biggest pier.
Every hotel five stars it is
And oh, the music, it's as cool as a fridge.
Every shop sells stuff for free,
And it has the best tea.
At night it's peace, just peace
And in the day there are no rules.
The epic Joe a famous man
The epic Joe, a famous building.
Joe Land is in the sun
But it all started from a little rocket
Joe Land is all luxury cars
That have sofas in stead of seats!
The most played sport is foot rug
As you can guess
Football mixed with rugby.

Joe Johnson (9)
All Saints East Clevedon CE Primary, Clevedon

Florence Land

In Florence Land pharaohs rule.
It's a world I dreamt up where everything is true.
This is a picture of me, a royal beauty to see.
Never a tear in my eye, however people say I cry.
My second in command is Duck,
Even though he prefers lovely muck.
I have a pool made for him
So he can splash, dive and swim.
You should come and visit one day
And then you can say to all your friends and family
To now officially visit me.
For even though the doors protest
And my guards are as fierce as a storm,
I am gentle, kind and warm.

Florence Bushby (9)
All Saints East Clevedon CE Primary, Clevedon

Once Upon A Dream

I made a poem that I thought was great
That the people that were judging would appreciate,
I really hoped that I'd do good
Because my classmates said that I definitely should,
I put my poem in the competition
Because my lovely teacher gave me permission,
I entered my poem in Once Upon A Dream
Because I bet it hit the judges like a laser beam,
Of course my poem is the best
Because it definitely hit them like lemon zest.
I can't believe I got a cool book token
And I'll make sure this dream will never be broken.

Isaac James Anthony Brown (9)
All Saints East Clevedon CE Primary, Clevedon

Joie's Adventures

When I am older I'm going to live on a farm
with pigs in the back barn.
In my spare time, I will write
and draw in the moonlight.
In my books I will write adventure stories
with *boom! Crash!* and *bang!*
And when I'm on my farm I will always have a lovely smile
like the happiest butterfly.
All my animals will get used to me
and I will get used to them.
In the night I will look up at the moon
smiling down on me
and think how lucky I am.

Joie Pauline Joy Archer-Haggerty (9)
All Saints East Clevedon CE Primary, Clevedon

To My Great Brothers

Have fun on the waves
Have fun on the sea
Meet people who are nice as can be.
I will have your back
Wherever you go
As long as you do not go.
Now you know that too
Stay with me, 'cause you're all I need
Just always have fun
'Cause you're the best and the leader.
We have had great times
But goodbye I will never forget you.

Tillie Megan Thomas (9)
All Saints East Clevedon CE Primary, Clevedon

Animals

Animals are cute, animals are fun
They play around in the hot warm sun.
Once I met one in the street
It had very, very furry feet.
I said, 'It's nice to meet you,
Why don't you come round my house
And eat a bowl of stew.'
The animal said, 'Thank you for my stew,
It's lovely to have met you.'

Olivia Phoenix (8)
All Saints East Clevedon CE Primary, Clevedon

Butterfly

I wish, I wish I could fly higher and higher in the sky
Like a butterfly.
Up above the trees.
Playing with the tiny bees.
My wings would be big and bold
They could hold me in the wildest storm.
I could stay up till dawn
I wish, I wish I could fly higher and higher in the sky
Like a butterfly.

Elsie Fay Barzotelli (8)
All Saints East Clevedon CE Primary, Clevedon

Grace's Griffin

Once I met a griffin.
It was as scared as can be.
I found it a nice hiding place up in a tree.
The griffin was clever and flew up to me
And said, 'I'm a griffin and so are you!
Hop on my back and we will race.'
Then I said, 'Ace!'

Grace Griffin (8)
All Saints East Clevedon CE Primary, Clevedon

My Dream World

In my dream world
Massive flying cakes catapult marshmallows
in your mouth at rapid fire.
Everybody lives in fifty metre tall cupcakes
And owns a hoverboard.
And a spaceship
With chocolate mousse launchers.
Also the trees are made out of candyfloss.

Fraser Heysham (9)
All Saints East Clevedon CE Primary, Clevedon

Animals

Animals, animals, they're so fun
They scratch but so much fun!
I push you round near my gran's
In a pink flowery pram.
And I filmed it on a cam in a pram.
Near B&Ms we stopped to have a look inside
And got some Dreamies then ran back home.

Jasmine Bailey (9)
All Saints East Clevedon CE Primary, Clevedon

The Magic Football Boot

The football boot is as good as Messi
It walks on its own and scores lots of goals.
The football boot runs as fast as a cheetah.
It races across the pitch like Sánchez.
The football boot runs through mud
And gets very dirty digging up the mud.

Jack Nash (8)
All Saints East Clevedon CE Primary, Clevedon

Rainbow Ninja

You're the rainbow ninja
Everyone must obey
Like a lion ruling the Savannah
All through the day
Time flies when you're ninjas of the night
One green, one black, one blue
And then there's you.

Ned Redford (9)
All Saints East Clevedon CE Primary, Clevedon

Untitled

Imagine a penalty *boom*, *bash*, goal
Just get the shiniest boots
Imagine a stadium as big as two classrooms
Just think a ref shows a red card to the best
Just get the best football vest.

Teddy Birkbeck (8)
All Saints East Clevedon CE Primary, Clevedon

Untitled

Animals
'Do you love animals?'
Said the cat nervously.
I love them. Animals, animals
Some are cuddly and some are scratchy,
Some are bouncy.
If you had a pet, what would it be?

Kitty Surendranath (8)
All Saints East Clevedon CE Primary, Clevedon

Ice Cream

Ice creams are delicious
Ice creams are fun
There are lots
of different
flavours to eat
Chocolate,
Caramel,
Vanilla,
Toffee,
Coffee,
All are
Nice to
eat.

Isabelle Abrahams (8)

All Saints East Clevedon CE Primary, Clevedon

Believe

So you wanna be a star?
Burning bright like the sun.
Every little star is shining on you.
But you just don't know it yet.
Someday you will know it.
How about now?

Charlie Andrew Yull (8)
All Saints East Clevedon CE Primary, Clevedon

Untitled

In my dream world there are houses made of chocolate
Beds made out of teddy bears
The rain is fizzy Coke
Any animal you can imagine
Will appear right in front of you.

Freyja Ridge (8)
All Saints East Clevedon CE Primary, Clevedon

Sparkles

Oh Sparkles, where have you been,
This time I've been waiting,
To hop on your glorious stride,
Me on my own alone,
Waiting for your appearance
My best friend is here,
Now we can take that glide,
Your horn sparkles,
Dashing up through the night sky,
To see the wonderful tribe,
Bouncing, floating, gliding,
Until the sun rises,
Dashes of colour came to me.
Oh Dasher,
It's you.
Sparkles' mum.
I swear I've seen you before,
Oh Sparkles,
Where are you?
Another day long,
Until the moon rises,
Once again,
I can't wait for another adventure,
Tears started to build up,

I'm bored,
It's only been a second,
What to do now,
I've started to wait,
You didn't turn up
Where are you?
Are you there?
I waited for you again,
Guess what?
We're not friends,
Never,
I will definitely miss you,
Your glowing horn,
You sparkling in the night sky
I started to tear
A wet tear
Down my cheek
I will miss you
Sparkles,
Are you still here?
It's been ten years,
Do you remember me?
I remember you,
That night
I joined her again

I shall never be so happy,
No one will ever replace you,
Sparkles,
I love you,
Do you?
I'm not five now,
I'm fifteen.
One thing Sparkles,
Can you remember me forever?
Because I will.

Lauren Rose Baber (9)
Barley Close Community Primary, Mangotsfield

Dreams

I had a dream about playing for Chelsea
Against Manchester United in the Champions League
Final
Walking out onto the extensive pitch
Deafening fans screaming my name
Amongst some of the best players in the world
The referee blew his whistle.

I sprint towards the ball
The successful player beside me
A player in red sprints past me
He crosses it in... *Goal!*
I was devastated.

A player kicked me the ball at kick-off
I ran down the line and had a shot...
Goal! The crowd went wild
My team came and celebrated with me.
This was the most exciting moment in my career.

The referee blew his whistle for half time.
My team came together
They all congratulated me
I was proud of myself
I felt like a million pounds.

Rhys Perry (10)
Barley Close Community Primary, Mangotsfield

Once Upon A Dream

I'm walking on a bridge where no one's been,
It says it's haunted,
How do they know?
They don't know I'm sure.

I'm running on a bridge where no one's been,
There's a hole in the bridge who did it?
How do I get across, this is the end is it not?
Who knows?
There's a whisper whose voice is it, who knows?
Is it a ghost? Is it human?

I'm jogging on a bridge,
There's a chest is it a real one or is it a trap?
I should open it,
I opened it,
There's money, I'm rich
I picked it up.

Oh no

Now I'm falling down a hole, will it end?
Where will it take me?
I don't know, it seems like forever -
Wait, the hole is getting smaller.

I'm getting stuck, will I be trapped forever?
I finally make it down,
Waiting, I'm in a cage, a man
He started talking,
He told me,
I will be haunted forever,
He wouldn't let me go.

I'm lonely, what should I do?
Will someone rescue me?
I tried to escape,
But,
The near to death meter grew and grew,
I was one bar away,
I don't want to get killed.
No I don't.
I'm worried,
Then the man came,
He counted,
three, two, one.
Any minute I will be dead,
The meter was full,
Would I survive?
I was dead.

Gracie Barter (9)
Barley Close Community Primary, Mangotsfield

Proper Equestrian

On my thoroughbred,
Flying up into the sky,
Reaching for the gold,
Yet a dream to unfold!

That medal I want,
That I achieved for showjumping,
On my animal that weighs a tonne.
Preparing myself,
With that photo on my shelf!

I want the glory,
The big finish,
With my friend,
My companion,
My dream horse that really flies!

A dream never dies,
Especially mine,
Because my fine dream will come true!
Let's just take a chance,
With a magnificent pace,
Ready to race for the gold!

Crowds start cheering,
As we land the highest jump,
Standing at one metre and ninety-five centimetres!

That was hard,
But we made it!
An Olympic showjumper on a thoroughbred.
Winning the gold medal!

Supporting Great Britain,
Leading Britain's fate,
Also taking the bait!

Crowds go ballistic,
Cameras pointing at us in every angle!
But...
A dream not to tangle.

We are famous!
Yet my horse is happy.
Because he finally gets the glory.

All that time.
We thought we wasted,
But was like a bite of a lime.

Now that's what I call a...
A proper equestrian,
Winning the Olympics for showjumping.

Lillyanna Golding (10)
Barley Close Community Primary, Mangotsfield

The Dream Match

As I was getting ready for the final,
Was I ready to face some of the best,
Or was I not?
I started to warm-up,
Will I score or will I let down the team?

The small children had come,
They were in little Manchester United football kits,
All of a sudden a little boy had come to hold my hand,
Suddenly we started walking out,
Manchester City was already there.

Now it was time for kick-off,
Manchester City had to start,
Lingard quickly took the ball off Agüero,
And paced down the wing and crossed it.
Pogba chested it and passed it to me
And I finished it.

It was eighty-nine minutes in,
Then ninetieth minute Pogba scored
We had won.

Adnan Mustafa (10)
Barley Close Community Primary, Mangotsfield

Nightmare Child

One small five-year-old,
Can be very bold,
No one knows,
What's behind those frills and bows,
You're about to find out,
How much little ones pout.

My cruel sister,
Gave me a blister,
'An accident,' she said to Mummy,
Little does she know, I have proof, that little dummy,
But oh no, she's both wicked and smart,
Her acting is a piece of art.

Things only got worse,
She took my purse,
She's taken all my money,
Now this really isn't funny,
She took all my lipstick too,
And flushed it down the loo.

She cut up all of my clothes,
She's definitely on the top of my List of Foes,
Took my computer and phone,
She really means business, down to the bone,

I'm half bald now,
I never knew how strong she was. Ow!

Wait a second,
What is this?
My hair is fair,
My stuff is all there,
Phew, it was just a terrible nightmare,
But oh dear,
My real little sister is yelling in my ear.

Harriet Daisy Vickers-Graham (10)
Barley Close Community Primary, Mangotsfield

In My Nightmare

In my dreams,
I could be a doctor,
A doctor that saves lives,
In my dreams.

In my dreams,
I could be a fire lady,
A fire lady putting out treacherous fires,
In my dreams.

In my dreams,
I could be a police lady,
A police lady that exhibits no restraint,
In my dreams.

In my dreams,
I could be a teacher,
A teacher that educates the young minds of children,
In my dreams.

In my dreams,
I could be a wolf,
A wolf fiercely stalking its prey,
In my dreams.

In my dreams,
I could be a unicorn,
A unicorn that soars across the sky
Bringing everyone to safety,
In my dreams.

In my nightmare,
I could be a helpless citizen,
A helpless citizen drowning in darkness,
In my nightmare.

Isla Honey Fidler (10)
Barley Close Community Primary, Mangotsfield

My Dream

A day like the mist
Horrible and cold
On a boat it's called the Titanic
Praying that I won't get the same fate
For when I realised the name
Hope going through my organs,
I wanted to leave but it was too late
Five minutes in I wanted to leave
I'm horrified every time I look at the sea
Going in the first-aid room
Wondering what's in there
Then I saw blue bodies everywhere
Daring not to touch one
I don't know why but I did
Then they all tried to attack me!
I rushed out then, closing the door
The floor slippery
Falling all over the place
Then I saw a crack in the wall
The boat's sinking!
Then I was falling
Falling through the crack

'Help, help!'
I was shouting
But it was no use
I'm with sea...

Ethan John Moran (10)
Barley Close Community Primary, Mangotsfield

The Whale

Sailing across the vast ocean,
With the whales and fish,
Nothing to eat or drink,
Except for a salad dish,
Everything was boring and dull,
Bored was my skull,
Until down, down, down I went,
And to my surprise,
Then I saw a whale in front of my eye.
His body was big, his neck was too,
Who knew what this thing could do?
'Hello,' the whale said,
'Why don't you jump on my head?'
So on I get,
We swim out into the blue,
It's a beautiful place
Don't you think so too?'
We saw brightly coloured fish,
The whale ate one and said, 'Delish!
Now it's time to go,' he said,
And I opened my eyes,
I was in bed.

Benjamin Norman (10)
Barley Close Community Primary, Mangotsfield

Cup Final Dream

In my sleep, I was in the cup final,
It was Manchester United Vs Chelsea,
When it was half-time, guess what?
The score was seven to four,
Manchester United was winning by three and Chelsea had four.
Now it was seven to five, two more goals for Chelsea.
Then they would be top!
Seven to six, one more goal.
Eden Hazard scored four,
John Terry scored one,
Oscar scored one,
On Manchester United it was Rashford three,
Mkhitaryan four,
Because it was seven all now it went to penalty.
I scored and guess who won, it wasn't Chelsea it was Manchester United.

Zack Yeandel (10)
Barley Close Community Primary, Mangotsfield

Once Upon A Dream

I'm a wild cat, free,
My fur flows in the wind,
I caught a mouse nice and juicy,
The taste of delicious blood in my mouth.

I'm a wild cat, free,
My ears big and strong,
I fight for my clan,
I deserve this life.

I'm a wild cat, free,
I lived for this long,
Why stop now,
I love this life.

I'm a wild cat, free,
I have all this food,
Why do I share
I cannot resist,
I need more,
I'm a wild cat, free,
I'm vivid and free,
I'm a wild cat, free.

Amelia Livingstone (10)
Barley Close Community Primary, Mangotsfield

Once Upon A Dream

Once upon a dream,
The dragons,
The fierce, fire-breathing dragons,
Fought fairies,
Once upon a dream,
The fairies,
The magic, elegant fairies,
Fought dragons.
Once upon a dream,
The Super S,
The amazing, powerful Super S,
Brought peace between fairies and dragons.
Once upon a dream,
The flowers spread,
The trees grew,
Happiness flew,
Once upon a dream,
The fairies had a princess.
Once upon a dream,
The dragons had a prince.
Once upon a dream,
Super S saved magic.
Once upon a dream.

Lillia Rose Clarke (10)
Barley Close Community Primary, Mangotsfield

The Creepy House

I dreamed that I was in a huge house,
I saw a girl,
She touched me and I ran outside,
Outside was a zombie,
A fast, frightening zombie,
So I ran back inside!

I went to a boy's bedroom,
I looked around,
The girl wasn't there,
I was safe,
Safe like being in my own bedroom,
The girl wasn't here.

Out through the wall came a ghost,
I hid in silence,
It came closer,
I left the house,
The tall, creaky house,
Ready for my next adventure.

Matty Fenlon (9)
Barley Close Community Primary, Mangotsfield

Dreams

I had a dream,
That I would get a pet unicorn.
It was cute and cuddly,
Her name was Poppy,
She had a gold, glittery horn,
She also had a rainbow, furry mane,
She also had white furry fur,
I had a dream
Poppy would fly me across the world,
We would feast on jelly beans,
I had a dream
We would cuddle up by a campfire,
When we woke up in the morning we ate
Candyfloss grass,
We also ate lolly trees.
We also ate gummy bear bushes,
I had a dream.

Summermay Johnson (10)
Barley Close Community Primary, Mangotsfield

The Silly Beano

In my dream I saw,
Said the Beano to Dennis,
What is that
Walter doing behind Dennis?
Oh what is he doing there
Oh why?
Said the Beano to Dennis.

Said the Beano to Dennis,
Oh teach me to be a menace,
Oh please do,
Please,
Oh please do,
Said the Beano to Dennis.

Said the Beano to Dennis,
Oh please let me be a menace,
Oh please do...

Cormack Walsh (10)
Barley Close Community Primary, Mangotsfield

My Superhero

My superhero is my dad
I think he is so great
We fly so high and I don't exaggerate
But there's something special about my dad
That I've never had, apart from a dad, he's my best lad!

We're superheroes in the shadows,
Waiting for our call, standing there proud and tall.
With a base like a wall, we fight, save and inspire.
So you'd better believe it all!

Tyrell Henry (11)
Barley Close Community Primary, Mangotsfield

Noises In My Room

With the sound of the central heating
And the music beating,
I hear the sound of cars beeping,
Scratching on my wall,
All goes dark,
All goes bare,
All noises start getting louder and louder
It gives me a scare
Next to my desk
Tapping,
Banging,
I wait and I wait
I wait for my fear to come,
But it comes and goes,
It gives me a fright.

Mya Hawkins (10)
Barley Close Community Primary, Mangotsfield

A Boy On The Hill

Once upon a dream,
A nightmare struck,
A boy with one thought and one life,
The thought was to kill and take it from them.

The boy lived on the hill,
Where no one paid a bill,
Where the floors
Had no doors,
To go through.

The nightmare starts,
When lightning strikes the hill,
His dream is to kill and have bad thoughts.

Ellie Bowen (10)
Barley Close Community Primary, Mangotsfield

My Dream

Zoom, zoom! She out-skills the best players.
Daniel, Rhys and Tahar try to slide-tackle.
She trips.
'Kick!'
'Hobbs you tack,' Luca was nice.
'OK'
'Oooooh Hobbs is tackling it.'
Harrison is the goalie.
Hobbs shoots and scores
'Ha, ha, ha, ha, ha, ha!'
Hobbs does a backflip.
We won the World Cup!

Billie Mae Hobbs (9)
Barley Close Community Primary, Mangotsfield

Cake

Chocolate cake is so tasty
Pineapple cake is so good
All I eat and bake
Is pineapple and chocolate cake
So I saved the best for last
Carrot and thyme cake.

Ellis Sealey (10)
Barley Close Community Primary, Mangotsfield

The Daydream

My, my, my, this horrible history lesson is dreary,
I decided to drift off, for I am really weary,
Suddenly, my mysterious mind transports me,
Into a new unknown world, how can this be?
Swaying from side to side,
I lose my balance on this rocky ride,
Raspy voices, hearing aggressive shouts,
I can't he's trying to make out,
I open my eyes and see before me,
An ugly sea captain as ugly as the scab on my knee,
He looks at me with his ugly glare,
I stand my ground, I try to scare,
I find myself on this boat,
(The one I was on could hardly float),
I get sucked by a twisty tornado,
Eventually saved by a man called Ado,
Who invites me to this royal party,
Could be a little arty!
Is there someone snoring?
I would be surprised, it's really boring!
Interested, I climb on a mysterious red tail,
I feel its slimy but relaxing scales,
I suddenly hear a hair-raising roar,
The dragon scraping its sharp claws,

I open my eyes, a little stubborn to be awake.
A lot of trouble is at stake!
I realise it's Miss Screecher,
The horrible history teacher.

Ramla Ilyas (10)
Barton Hill Academy, Bristol

Dragon City

D ragon City is finally in my sight
R unning faster until I see the light
A dragon greets me as I approach the gate
G oing in I hope I'm not late
O n my way to the dragon's den now
N ow that I'm here I greet him with a bow.

'C an we be friends?' he asks with a smile
I didn't want to keep him waiting a while
'T hat would be great to be your friend,'
'Y ahoo,' he said. 'Let's go to the den.'

Kyrese Wood (9)
Barton Hill Academy, Bristol

What Is A Dream?

Every night I ponder,
To answer all my wonders,
But there is one I don't understand.
Am I living in a Dreamland?
What is a dream?

They come in every sort of theme,
Some you don't want to end,
Others you don't want to see again!
Sometimes they seem so real,
It will make you squeal.
That still doesn't answer my question,
Are dreams real?

Do unicorns exist?
Please tell me, I insist.
Well I'll never know,
At least it's not you though.

Fatou Jagne (10)
Barton Hill Academy, Bristol

Fun Day

All I dream about is this cool mysterious place.
All I see is people playing around the place.
Me and my cousins went ice skating to have a fun day.
All the people screaming and having lots of fun.
This is how to end the exciting cool place.
The hot sun is shining on everyone today.
Everyone is getting ice cream to cool themselves today.
We all went to jump in the lake to cool ourselves from
the hot sunny day.
The fun day made us hungry and so we decided to
have lunch.

Sumaya Omar (10)
Barton Hill Academy, Bristol

Night And Nature Left Me

Dance beneath the stars,
As you sleep in the night.
Let the thunder overtake you,
As lightning fills the sky.
Feel the force of nature,
Penetrate your skin.
Spin with the world,
As the magic sinks in.

The moon split in half,
As the stars crumbled.
Falling like fireworks into the sea,
I watched my world
Fall apart the day
My nature left me.

Rayan Mahammoud Ali (10)
Barton Hill Academy, Bristol

My Perfect Dream

I'd love a unicorn you see,
Not for anyone else, but just for me.
It would have to be white with bright pink hair and I
would ride it anywhere I dare.
I dream about unicorns when I am asleep,
It is more interesting than counting sheep.
They are prettier and more magical to behold,
At least that is what I have been told.
They can sweep you off your feet and fly,
Very high up above the clouds in the sky.
In my dreams I am alone,
Far, far away from anyone at home.
Sitting on my unicorn's back holding on tight.
He flaps his wings with all his might.
When I am flying alone at night,
I dream that everything in the world is right.
I only come back down to rest on my bed,
When I hear Mummy calling, 'Wake up sleepy head!'

Tia Paige Hansford (8)
Bridport Primary School, Bridport

Cake And Villains

Stampy likes to bake cake, he loves it.
To his heart he says to Lee, 'Bakery time!'
And so they go to the bakery.
Much as he loves cake Stampy ate bread.
'Poo!' he said. 'It tastes disgusting,'
Lea ate some cake.
'Fun!' he said, then a strange man was there,
'Ahhh!' said Stampy, it was Hit the Target.
'Noo,' said Lee, Hit the Target was a villain.
'Do this!' he said. Stampy pulled out a sword.
'Lucky you,' said Hit the Target. Stampy hit him.
Eye Spy said, 'Hit the Target,' but before he could
Eye Spy, a flying enemy, Stampy flung him in the air.

Chandler Gumbril (9)
Bridport Primary School, Bridport

Me, The Queen And The Zebracorn

I'm flying over America, I see,
With a zebracorn and the Queen,
Oh, look, an astronaut, on a pirate's ship,
Oh, and look over there, pirates by a launch pad.
It's the strangest thing I've ever seen
Look at the rocket, it's taking off.
With pirates inside.
Quick astronaut, catch up with those pirates,
In their ship in the big, wide ocean.
Come on guys, let's take a closer look!
I said as the rocket zoomed across the sky
Then I woke up and knew it was just a dream
And hoped that it would come true.

Daisy Johnson (8)
Bridport Primary School, Bridport

Evil Entertainers

S care was in the air,

C are not did clowns even if they could not bare

A sound that kills your ears,

R un you try, but it all comes to tears,

Y ou want to go but they drag you in.

N othing you can do to stop them.

I n your nightmare house they have you by the stem,

G oing somewhere, I think not.

H urt or not, you can make it back.

T o my reader, don't be scared when you're in my horror land.

Danielle Jones (9)
Bridport Primary School, Bridport

Dragons Vs Humans

A hot breeze filled the forest,
As dragons breathed fiery air,
The dragon king throws fireballs,
At the terrified humans,
That's us!
Daddy takes out his sword,
And cuts dragons' heads off,
Then Mummy takes out her belt,
And whips a dragon's wing,
My sister takes out her pencil,
And stabs a dragon's eye.
I pull a dagger out of my pocket,
And I throw it at the dragons,
At last the humans take victory,
Against the evil dragons.

Bradley Wilkinson (8)
Bridport Primary School, Bridport

Famous Fighters

One day in May,
I went to an arena,
And I saw Famous Fighters,
Some ninjas, some boxers drinking Ribena.

The Famous Fighters are big and bad,
They have tattoos all over,
They also have boxing gloves like they own them
Bruce Lee was fighting Muhammad Ali.
Chuck Norris was beating Jackie Chan.
Mike Tyson bit off Evander Holyfield's ear
Which was very bad!
But my mum came in and beat them all.
How cool!

Ruby Mary McLaughlin (9)
Bridport Primary School, Bridport

Candy Land

C andy is all around

A n adventure can be found

N ice cotton candy clouds in the sky

D own on the ground a rainbow unicorn walks by

Y ou can see Waddles the tortoise, he's made of gummy

L ollipop trees taste really yummy

A river of melted chocolate flows

N eon strawberry lace grass grows

D reams of candy can come true and I hope your dreams come true too.

Evie Moss (9)

Bridport Primary School, Bridport

The Duet With James

Gracefully spinning, turning and dancing
Performing a duet with my partner James.
Across the floor we move together.
A thousand steps whirl in my mind.
He moves me, I fly, he swings me, I slide.
Feeling like a rhythm, losing ourselves in our
dreamworld.
The crowd looks on, they cheer and shout.
Their faces a blur as we spin around.
The music slows, our dance is ending.
Sweating and panting, we collapse on the floor.

Grace Braddock (9)
Bridport Primary School, Bridport

Magical Forest

M y little forest lay there;
A nimals gather round me,
G laring sunrise in the morning,
I lay there to stay;
C almly I stroll,
A nother time;
L ight shines in the sunrise.

F orever and on it stays;
O kay as I stay under a tree,
R ain falls,
E very noon;
S unset goes down,
T ime after time.

Ella-Mae Rescorla (9)
Bridport Primary School, Bridport

Sweet Dreams

S ugar Land, let's go:
W ow it's so colourful here,
E at all the candy you can.
E xcellent idea,
T ake candy with you.

D rama Miss Unicorn got hit in the face,
R aining shelter!
E at the shelter,
A lso use cocktail umbrellas.
M ustn't drink the cocktail!
S eriously, that dream was sweet.

Ava Stordy (8)
Bridport Primary School, Bridport

Dragons

D o you hear him swooping and flying across the sky.

R oaming, flying creature like a king.

A nd does he look friendly? Does he look grotesque?

G reat big razor-sharp teeth does he have? Maybe.

O n and on he flies searching for that meal.

N o he might always play tricks to get away from humans.

S ometimes always thinking that humans are killers.

Toby Williams (9)
Bridport Primary School, Bridport

Fire, Fire In My House!

Red-hot fire is spreading through the house,
Eating its way to my door,
Downstairs the fire is wrecking the place.

'Help! Help!' everyone's shouting,
One not two, nobody noticed,
The fire was almost there.

Fire, fire is spreading,
I am worried and scared,
Really close the fire is getting,
Eventually I wake up but it was only a dream.

Chloe Ann West (8)
Bridport Primary School, Bridport

Unicorns

U nder and over the mythical trees,
N owhere to be seen deep in the forest of an
adventure,
I n a land where unicorns fly high.
C ome and explore the wonderful land of unicorns.
O ver meandering rivers and under bridges,
R unning along beside them, just me.
N o one but me and my unicorn friends,
S omewhere in Unicorn Land.

Lois Hodge (9)

Bridport Primary School, Bridport

My Dream

My name is Joe,
I am off to do my show
I take my path
Ready for the audience to laugh.

I am stuntman and king
Act as a joker in the circus ring
All applaud then I fly
Over heads in the sky.

Add faith
And it becomes a belief
Add action
And it becomes part of life
Add patience and time
And it ends with a dream.

Danny Mike Parkinson (9)
Bridport Primary School, Bridport

Sad Little House

I am broken
I am sad
I am looking very bad.

I smell earthy and rotten,
I know I have been forgotten.

I hear nothing,
I'm so lonely,
I need a family to own me.

Splash of paint,
Bit of fixing is all I need,
To get me glowing,

I am broken,
I am sad,
I'm looking very bad.

Jade Joy (8)
Bridport Primary School, Bridport

The Dream Pony

When I go to bed at night,
I snuggle down, turn off the light,
Hoping that the dream pony might
Light up the stars and make them bright.
When she comes to my delight,
With her mane and tail a pearly white.
She really is a lovely sight.
As I dream, my eyes shut tight
She winks at me and takes flight.
Chasing nightmares into the morning light.

Evie Fay Baker (9)
Bridport Primary School, Bridport

A Dream Of Springtime Colours

Hello daffodils,
Orange, yellow, white,
Dancing in your dresses,
Pretty, frilly, light.

Welcome crocuses,
Purple, white and gold,
Tiny, pearly snowdrops,
Early, brave and bold.

I love the colours in springtime,
As we leave winter behind,
The warmth and beauty of new growths,
Make the world seem very kind.

Laura Devine (9)
Bridport Primary School, Bridport

Mr Tiger

M r Tiger prowling through the dense forest
R eady to pounce on his prey.

T argeting his next victim
I stand there horrified without saying any words
G rowling ferociously he attacked the stunned deer.
E ating as though he was starving to death.
R ight where I stood I knew it was no ordinary dream.

Eliza Burt (9)
Bridport Primary School, Bridport

The Fairies And The Unicorn!

The night sky with glitz and glamour,
Shining stars finding a way,
Here comes a fairy,
She was in the sky with rainbow clouds of dust,
Later that day her fairy friends came and the unicorn
I feel magical with my unicorn fairy dust.
They fly away with power
They returned to a magical universe
With magical rainbows and a haul of treasure.

Sadie Faye Roach (8)
Bridport Primary School, Bridport

My Life As A Unicorn

Hello, my unicorn family,
I hope you don't mind a dog and a cat,
I brought them with me.
I've always wanted to be a unicorn.
Ever since I was little.
At first I thought my house was made of candy.
All my teachers and friends say that I'm insane about unicorns.
All different kinds,
Life isn't all cupcakes and rainbows.

Abigail Carter (9)
Bridport Primary School, Bridport

Liverpool Win The Semi-Final

I am feeling amazing,
Sat in a real football stadium,
Watching my favourite team.

Mum and Dad feeling sad,
Man United score a goal.

More and more cheer,
Supporting my team,
Liverpool score again,
Again, again and again,
My favourite team,
Win the semi-final,
Feeling over the moon.

Yousef Akka (9)
Bridport Primary School, Bridport

Race Cars

R ace cars get ready
A s the race is steady
C ars revving their engines
E xcited crowds are cheering.

C orners are nearing
A s the cars plunge round the track
R oaring cars are going fast.
S urprisingly, I wake from my dreams. Quickly, let's go back.

Oliver Bowditch (9)
Bridport Primary School, Bridport

The City Of Dragons

I moved into a new city that was magic.
But it might also mean it's tragic!
Dragons fly at night over the city,
I wonder why they act like they're eighty.
Lights go on at night,
Over the city I hear weird noises,
I think they're in a fight.
Now I feel very special.
But I'm still very careful.

Kalia Topaz Bracey (9)
Bridport Primary School, Bridport

Greg The Chilli Thief

A ginger fat,
A tough old cat,
He sings a battle song,
As other cats run along.

My dad's chilli plant,
On the window sill,
Greg sits in his basket
Underneath.

Greg reaches up,
On his two hind legs,
Two paws grab
And the little red dagger
Falls into the basket.

Xan Staal (8)
Bridport Primary School, Bridport

Me = F1

F orever in my dreams

O ccupying the cockpit of this F1 machine.

R eally excites me

M aybe I'll win a trophy!

U nexpectedly I line up right beside...

L ewis Hamilton

A round of applause for the champion

O h

N o

E nd of dream.

Joshua Paul Harper (9)
Bridport Primary School, Bridport

French Teacher

Who's my French teacher today?
What am I going to do today?
Am I going to go on a trip today?

I've got a French teacher who is Miss Pengon
Will she make a list of French numbers to learn,
Or make us write French sentences?
Who knows what will happen?
Who is my French teacher today?

Abigail Record (8)
Bridport Primary School, Bridport

Pig Poem

There is a pig called Ellie,
She is small and sometimes smelly,
She loves to have a bath,
And plays with a toy giraffe,
She snores when she is asleep,
And snorts when she is awake.
And she loves to go on a walk,
She also loves puddles,
And lots of cuddles.
I love Ellie and Ellie loves me!

Lily Stantiford (9)
Bridport Primary School, Bridport

Fairy Land

Fairies, fairies, shine so bright,
In the sparkling sky at night,
Bouncing, bouncing, bouncing ball,
Flying through the air,
The evil fairy queen takes over,
Stealing our fairy wands,
Feeling sad, fairy friend, think of a plan,
Fairy wands are back with us,
The evil queen no more.

Salma Akka (9)
Bridport Primary School, Bridport

Lost

Everyone is gone, no one is there
Except the trees and the leaves
The only sound is the chirping
Of birds flying above,
Looking down on my world.

As the light turns to darkness
The clouds start to fade
In their place is a shining star
I feel like I am in a dream.

Gala Nickels (9)
Bridport Primary School, Bridport

Dragons

D ragons can be different shapes, sizes and colours
R ed dragons are fire.
A lmost all dragons can fly.
G reen dragons cannot fly in the sky
O range dragons are baby fire dragons
N o fire dragon can fly in the rain.
S ome can only swim.

Jamie Oldershaw (9)
Bridport Primary School, Bridport

The Longest Jump Ever

Long jump is my favourite sport
On a Thursday night we meet
Near the end was my last jump
Going into the stadium I got wet

Jumped so far that I won
Up so far there was a crowd
My shoes had lots of sand
Prizes were won and my team were proud.

Ryan Burt (9)
Bridport Primary School, Bridport

Dragons

Dragons flying in the sky,
Dragons not sky high,
They can breathe fire,
Swoop in air,
Look around, dragons everywhere,

You may not believe,
But if you receive,
The magic keys,
I'm sure you'll believe.

Dragons.

Fred Battersby (9)
Bridport Primary School, Bridport

Pure Imagination

Pure imagination is in your mind.
It makes the impossible possible,
The unthinkable, thinkable.
And the unimaginable, imaginable.
It's like a projector in your mind
Where you make your own movie
From fiction to non-fiction
It's your creation.

Perry Allen (9)
Bridport Primary School, Bridport

Dancer

D ancing like a controlled puppet.

A beautiful ballerina dazzles on the stage.

N o it's gone all wrong!

C leverly she carries on.

E veryone grins and cheers.

R evelling in the joy she continues.

Lily Mann (8)
Bridport Primary School, Bridport

Chocolate And Derek The Dragons

Chocolate and Derek are dragons,
Their skin has lots of patterns,
They are as warm as mittens,
And as cute as kittens.
Their claws
Are like swords
Smashing everything in their way
First to fly away.

Harry James Hawker (9)
Bridport Primary School, Bridport

Who Am I?

I swim around the deep blue sea,
I have a very scaly long tail,
I swim through the sea like a rocket,
I have all sorts of powers,
I am female.
Who do you think I am?

Summer Jorja Parsons (9)
Bridport Primary School, Bridport

Superpowers!

S uper speed like my PC
U nforgettable invisibility
P owers that may underestimate me
E vil eyes that can shoot laser beams
R eal superheroes act all beastly.
P lenty of powers can you see
O h my gosh don't test me
W eather control and...
E lectricity
R esurrection I can bright back zombies
S uper smart like Tony Starke.

Jamol Dare (12)
Brockworth Primary Academy, Brockworth

Dragons

I've got this dragon
In my soul
It makes this roaring sound when I turn it on.
I'm on the ground now
This dragon is chasing me
I need somewhere to hide
Anywhere I go it finds me
I can't hide any more
I need to slay it with my sword
It's hunting me down
I need to hurry
Tonight's the night
It's going down
I need to prepare for battle.

Jaquan Carmica Smith (11)
Brockworth Primary Academy, Brockworth

Weather Wizard

I am the Weather Wizard,
I will now show you my power,
I help the sun to shine,
And make the summer shower,
Keep secret what you see today,
Tell no one what you saw,
Otherwise I promise,
The rain on you will pour.

I am the Weather Wizard,
I can summon tsunamis.
I hate fire hazards,
That's also my hobby.
Beware, or you will be battered...

Filip Mihalik (11)
Brockworth Primary Academy, Brockworth

Clown, Clown

Clown, clown,
Please stay away
Please stay away for just one day
I see you here, I see you there,
What is going on with your crazy hair?
You have a red nose
You have a funny pose
But I don't really find it fair
Not just the kids for the adults too
Considering the adults paid for you.

Casey Thomas (11)
Brockworth Primary Academy, Brockworth

I Once Saw A Unicorn!

I once saw an animal
That looked quite magical.
It had an amazing bright mane
But gave my eyes quite a pain.
It gave a neigh and was on its way
I made a twist of my hand
And it came to my land.
With sparkles of gold
Its eyes shone bright
And I woke up to a picturesque sight.

Amelie Witts (11)
Brockworth Primary Academy, Brockworth

Untitled

Dream when you are happy
Don't dream if you are scared
Because you will dream about clowns
And dream who you are
And dream when you are alive
And don't dream when you are dead
Or you will die again.

Adrian Midlane (11)
Brockworth Primary Academy, Brockworth

My Friend

My friend
Is like love
Around my heart.

She is warm
Like sun when
She cuddles me.

She is cool
In the hot noon.

She is my friend
And I am her friend.

Lacey Ann Richardson (11)
Brockworth Primary Academy, Brockworth

In My Nightmare

In my nightmare...
I see a shadow come shooting past

I hear footsteps

I feel really scared.

In my terrifying nightmare...
I see bloody hands holding a knife

I hear screams
I feel drum noises vibrating
Death.
In my nightmare.

Edward Patrick Harry Parsons (10)
Deane Discovery Centre, Blagdon Hill

In My Nightmare

In my nightmare
I see blood-hungry vampires
I see the blood on their teeth
Bat-winged hands
Blood-filled mouths
In my nightmare I see bloody vampires
My eyes are frozen in neutral
My mouth is wet
My heart is pounding.

Wraith Haysom (11)
Deane Discovery Centre, Blagdon Hill

In My Nightmare

In my nightmare
I see demons
I hear footsteps creeping closer
I feel so scared my heart is bulging
In my scary nightmare
I see bloodthirsty demons
I hear high-pitched screams
I feel horrified
In my nightmare you die.

Charlie Teasdale (8)
Deane Discovery Centre, Blagdon Hill

In My Nightmare

In my nightmare...
I see villains and their
Grabbing wrinkly hands
Bloodshot-red eyes
Screaming mouths
In my nightmare...
I see villains and my
Eyes freeze and pause
My mouth screams
My heart stops.
In my nightmare.

Travis Norman (10)
Deane Discovery Centre, Blagdon Hill

Nightmare

In my nightmare...
I see demons and their
Bloody hands
Blood-filled eyes
Deadly mouths

In my nightmare...
I see black figures and
My eyes stare
My mouth takes a deep breath
My heart bangs
In my nightmare.

Ty Chick (9)
Deane Discovery Centre, Blagdon Hill

Unicorns!

I saw a unicorn fly way up high almost above the sky.
Another unicorn was pink which made me stop and think.
Because all the rest were purple.
Then suddenly a unicorn came down and put me on his back
He was only a baby, he could soar with wings.
We flew towards a sky island
It was the home of 100,000,000,000 Pegasus and unicorns.
I hopped onto the island and I saw rainbows and clouds.
I heard loud music and magic-like noises.
In the night I saw one moon and two shooting stars.
Everyone was asleep except me.
So I went and took a peek at all the houses.
There were tables and chairs.
In the morning a unicorn accidentally cast a spell that reflected in the well
And turned me into a unicorn
My special power was making it rain glitter.
One unicorn could sing beautifully
Fortunately a fairy from Fairy Isle reversed the spell
And took me back to my house, safe in bed.

Alisha Jannette Davies (8)
Ford Primary School, Ford

My Tea With The Queen

One night I went to sleep and had an awesome dream,
I dreamt I got invited to have tea with the Queen.
I woke up to a noise so I looked out of the window,
And saw a giant royal stretch limo.
We travelled to London, It was such a long way,
I was just so glad that I didn't have to pay.
I arrived at the palace at half past three,
Just in time to get ready for tea.
I was so excited, happy and skippy,
The Queen said, 'I'm just popping out to get us some chippy.'
I scoffed down my fish, chips and mushy peas,
The queen offered dessert and I said, 'Yes please!'
We had lots of jelly and lots of ice cream,
And that ends my dream of tea with the Queen.

Jensen Harrison (9)
Ford Primary School, Ford

Dragon Game

I stand upon a pitch of pink
We're on Pluto I start to think
There are dragons dressed in football gear
I can hear the other dragons begin to cheer.

One dragon falls to the ground
He lets out an awful sound.
For he's gone and hurt his knee,
The unicorn doctor comes to see!

The unicorn uses his special powers to help,
The dragon then stops his yelp
With a sneeze of fire he shows he's well
The unicorn says all is well.

The game continues, my dragon's back
He aimed at the goal with a final hack
Hooray! It's in, they have drawn,
But then I wake up and it is gone.

Christian Webber (9)
Ford Primary School, Ford

Me And My Unicorn

My unicorn is multicoloured
She flies up in the sky
We see her every day
And always very high.

Unicorns are real
And her name is Princess Dash
She lives in Cloud City
And passes us by in a flash.

She has a twisted golden horn
That shines upon her head
It glides through the fluffy clouds
On her way to bed.

Her wings are made of feathers
And she flaps them to and fro
The faster that she does this
The quicker she will go.

I love my unicorn so much
She always tries to do things right
Bathing with the dragons
In the darkness of night.

Jessica Lee (9)
Ford Primary School, Ford

My Dream Of Dogs

My dream of dogs: dogs of all kinds live here
Normal breeds, mixed breeds get along
Pedigree, even mongrels they get along.
Whether they're clean or scruffy
Some with pointy or floppy ears,
All dogs love to run and chase,
Let's see which ones will have a race.
Playing games of run and fetch
I wonder how long our legs are stretched?
Now I'm sitting here in deep thought,
I think now we all need a drink
Now we've had a game of fetch
Let's now see how long these leads will stretch
Now on the way home to rest,
With all these dogs around me,
I feel blessed.
Goodnight.

Tazmin Hopkins (9)
Ford Primary School, Ford

Dragons And Fire

I laid my head down to sleep,
And in my dream I start to creep.
All I could see was a deep dark shadow lurking by,
This made me want to cry.
As I gazed into the deep, dark night,
I saw something that gave me a fright.
Standing tall with bony knees
I shouted, 'Just don't hurt me please.'
A dragon charged at me with rings of fire
His claws were sharp and his hair like wire
I ran to a warehouse so nothing could find me
Inside it was stinky and very grimy
The dragon approached me with big blue eyes
So he must have heard my cries.

McKenzie James Bird (8)
Ford Primary School, Ford

Spring Camping

It's a wonderful day,
For camping in my tent
The green trees are swishing
And the pink hedgehogs are snuffling
I feel very happy!
Camping in my tent.

The birds are singing,
At sunrise
The world is coming alive!
It is spring,
The best time to camp
A brook's gurgling
Next to a stream
So it's a wonderful day!

Amy May Parmenter (8)
Ford Primary School, Ford

Danger In The Night

D arkness all around
R oaring of dragons everywhere
A dragon swoops down, blowing fire from its nose
G lowing buildings burn from the flames
O nto the next town, but who knows where
N ight falls, beware...!

Isabelle Jayne Hutton (9)
Ford Primary School, Ford

Messi

M essi is my bestie
E nthusiastic and clever
S killed and quick
S peciality is football
I s the best footballer ever.

Kobi Collins (9)
Ford Primary School, Ford

A Garden Horror!

Once upon a dream there was a bright garden,
That had a legend that told,
It was haunted by a weed-made lady,
It ended up being quite old.

It never ended well in the garden,
People went in and never came out,
I was thinking about going there,
But now it's sort of a doubt.

I was so tempted,
My hands were shaking,
I needed to go there,
My stress was making.

I've got a story about the lady,
Listen carefully, read it maybe.

'There was an old woman from Leeds
Who swallowed a packet of seeds,
And in less than an hour,
Her ears were a flower,
And her head was covered in weeds'.

Is that the end of my dream I wonder?
It must be because I woke from my slumber.

Sophie Artis (9)
Halberton Primary School, Halberton

The Unichicken

Every night I lie in bed,
Resting my precious head.

Every night I dream,
Like an electric beam.

It must be a dream,
It must be a dream.

Every night I dream about a chicken from Essex,
But now he lives in Wessex.

Everyone sees something about him,
That they use to doubt him.

He has a horn
Like a unicorn.

Everyone knows his name,
But not in the way of fame.

Everything went wrong for the unichicken,
They caught him doing lots of finger licking.

Everyone knows he went to jail,
His life was a big fail.

It was a dream,
It was a dream.

Poppy Sharland (10)
Halberton Primary School, Halberton

Untitled

I rest my head on the soft cushion of my bed,
As I snore,
My dreams start to roar,
I dream of a phoenix stood on a stone,
White wisps of snow as a throne,
She calls to the skies
And off she flies,
Her snowed claws soon disappear
Oh, nothing to fear,
Nothing to fear,
This dream starts to disappear,
Oh, what a dream,
Oh, what a dream,
My cushion, as soft as a feather,
Wakes me from my dream like Heather
Oh, what a dream,
Oh, what a gorgeous dream.

Freya May Davis (10)
Halberton Primary School, Halberton

The Premier League

Once there was a man,
With a ball at his feet,
His shot was weak.

He took the shot,
And looked at the plot,
It must be a dream?

Then he floated through space,
Seeing pizza,
With a box of chips,
It must be dream,

It must be a dream!
It must be a dream!
Then he woke up in the beautiful morning light.

Harry Lejeune (9)
Halberton Primary School, Halberton

A Girl's Dream

There once was a girl who had a dream
Who sat on a cloud and she was a queen
And she had a dream and she was very mean
She had a demon and he drank lots of tea
And he was very keen on having beans
So he sat on a tree and ate lots of beans.
And sardines with marching bees
Then I waited for my fantastic dream
With my sardines and a happy cup of marching bees
In my dreams.

Meisha Clapp (10)
Halberton Primary School, Halberton

On An Island

I had a dream, a weird dream
There was a man on a boat, cold and wet,
He landed on an island
He looked and looked
He tripped over a rock and landed in a cave,

He was tripping, slipping down the cave,
Running, jumping.
I saw a dragon steal lots of gold,
I got away face-to-face.

I jumped in my rich boat
Sailed away
What a rich day.

Rupert Awcock (9)
Halberton Primary School, Halberton

Untitled

I rest my head on my pillow,
As I snore my dreams start to soar,

I dream of fairies stood on a stone,
Golden sparks of magic as a throne,
They sing a song
To the sky,
And off they fly,
I see the tips of their wings
Soon disappear,
Oh what a dream,
Oh what a dream,
My cushion, soft as a feather wakes me.

Alicia Sugden (9)
Halberton Primary School, Halberton

Untitled

Every night I have a rest
I shut my eyes to rest

I wake up next to a train
It has to be a dream, a dream
It has to be a dream.

I went in a coach, it was amazing,
I was with my brothers, it was fun.
I had a good time, it was the funniest day ever,
Then I woke up in my bed in the morning.

James Elliott (9)
Halberton Primary School, Halberton

The Deep, Dark Woods

Lost
In the deep, dark woods
With my dog Tyson,
Then I saw a colourful Mickey Mouse,

He scared me,
I fell in a hole,
In there
Was nothing but then

I landed in a nice
Cosy bed, trying to make my
Dad believe me but he
Did not, so I went
To sleep and had
Another dream.

Millie Crane (9)
Halberton Primary School, Halberton

Lost

Lost,
In the deep, deep woods,
No longer in my warm bed,
It was not very good.

Cold and wet,
On my own,
No one there,
I bet.

Finally back home,
In my lovely cosy bed,
But telling my mum she would not believe me,
Saying it was all unknown.

Eden Jones (9)
Halberton Primary School, Halberton

A Dream

As I snore,
My dreams turn into galore.

I'm on the big, black stage,
Meant to be in a rage.

Playing on the football team,
This must be a brilliant dream!

I wake up in my bed,
Rub my eyes,
Feel my head
And smile.

Lola Hughes (9)
Halberton Primary School, Halberton

Pug On The Beach!

I had a dream bout my pug
I curled up in my bed, nice and snug
I dreamt that I was on the beach
With Lolly running round my feet
I threw a ball and Lolly ran
And instead of giving the ball to me,
She gave it to an old man.
Lolly then ran into the sea
She likes swimming just like me
Lolly came out soaking wet
Though I had to dry her since she is my pet
Next, we sat down and our picnic was done
But I looked over to Lolly and she didn't have anyone
So I said, 'Lolly, here you go, here's a treat.'
I bet you think it's very sweet
Then we got her a bow
And uh-oh!
It's six o'clock so we better go
That's my dream, did I hate it? No.

Kacy Lucas (8)
Milton Park Primary School, Weston-Super-Mare

A Random Dream

Nothing had prepared me to climb the mountain that I see,
I'm ready to climb it but I'm nervous as can be,
I see a small light,
But I shiver with fright,
I think it's a dragon about to bite,
What should I do, follow a kite?
What should I do, fall off a height?
Well I don't know what to do,
Should I think of something I drew?
I am up a mountain,
I see a cave,
I pull myself up feeling kind of brave,
I run into the cave, feeling that I'm about to be saved,
I see a small wizard,
He says I will be saved
I didn't know what that meant
I wasn't really sure,
But in the end, I felt like I was about to roar.

Patryk Gabriel Zapotoczny (9)
Milton Park Primary School, Weston-Super-Mare

I Ran Through The Forest

I ran through the forest
Not knowing what was wrong,
I looked back, to see if it was gone.
Roar!
I looked, there were only four,
I could see dragons soaring through the sky,
From down here, they looked very high;
The creatures were big and fat,
And on one's head, it carried a rat!

I ran through the forest,
Suddenly seeing a cottage,
And then on, I could smell sausage.
I opened the door and ran into the kitchen
And on the table I saw a kitten,
The kitten opened its mouth
To show six sharp teeth
Then it jumped to my feet...
Arghhhhh!

James Horlick (9)
Milton Park Primary School, Weston-Super-Mare

Bedtime!

Imagination, imagination!
Fairy tales and communication,
With strange creatures yet to discover,
While we dream under our bed covers.

If you see monsters, don't let them scare
You don't need to worry, they're not really there!
Most creatures are friendly, some of them are not
Now please remember that they are never forgot!

Now close your eyes and get some sleep
Before Mum and Dad come in and peek
Dream away and see the creatures
If you look closely, you can see their features.

George Richard Hartley (9)
Milton Park Primary School, Weston-Super-Mare

Footballer

F it and healthy is what you should be

O ffside is not what we want to see

O nside position is where it's at

T ackling with your feet and not a bat

B oots have to be worn; Reebok or Nike

A ttacking with skill, what a good strike

L inesman is watching you passing the ball

L eft winger comes forward and scores a great goal

E nergy needed for that goal celebration

R eferee blows his whistle, you're the hero of the nation.

Finlay Francis-Carter (9)
Milton Park Primary School, Weston-Super-Mare

Wonderland

W hat a place of dreams and mystery

O verlooking the arts of history

N ever-ending creatures and sorcery

D emanding attention of fun and forgery

E vil witches forge crafty spells

R usalla, a female water spirit, sits and dwells

L oathing her mermaid life and living

A waiting her knight for love and giving

N ow here are the fairies to bring peace and tranquillity

D emanding the witches came down with stability.

Alicia Bessant (8)

Milton Park Primary School, Weston-Super-Mare

Me And My Guards

Me and my guards work as a team
We work hard to defeat the bad
And being a knight in armour was always my dream
When our men are defeated, we are sad,
Protecting the castle is our job
The weapons we use are a sword and a shield
And we stop people from being robbed
Then after that, we practise on the field
Me and my guards think it's a happy time
The people in the village sing together
Some of them might mime
I hoped this dream would last forever.

Harry Tedder (9)
Milton Park Primary School, Weston-Super-Mare

I Dreamt, I Dreamt, I Dreamt

I dreamt my rabbits could fly,
Way up high in the sky,
They even had clothes on and one was wearing a tie
I also dreamt that parrots like carrots
And balloons like cartoons
Does snake eat cake or cake eat snake?
In the land of nod, I dreamt I had a fishing rod
On the land, there was a cat called Squeak
She liked playing hide 'n' seek
The sun shone on Jon, he had a kite
And off he went on his bike!
I dreamt, I dreamt, I dreamt.

Charlotte Louise Cooper (8)
Milton Park Primary School, Weston-Super-Mare

Under The Sea

In my dream, I imagine that I'm under the sea
The fish that pass by smile at me
I wonder where they're going, I wonder who they'll meet,
I wonder if they'll see a mermaid sitting on a seat!
Up above my head, I see dolphins jump and leap,
I wonder to myself, *where do all these sea creatures sleep?*
If I lived under the sea...
I would be a crab, scuttling happily.

Ruby Edwards (9)
Milton Park Primary School, Weston-Super-Mare

The Race

Bang! The race starts
Off I shoot
Past everyone
I'm in the lead
When someone overtakes me
I search within for more energy
Beads of sweat run down my face
My heart is racing
Banging at my ribcage
My legs power on
Propelling me forwards
The finish line is in sight
I crash through the ribbon
The crowd goes wild.

Jack Ford (9)
Milton Park Primary School, Weston-Super-Mare

My Nightmares!

Nightmares,
Nightmares,
So creepy,
Nightmares,
Nightmares,
Make me sleepy.
Here's some dreams I've had in my life.
Nightmares,
Nightmares,
Are so cruel,
Nightmares,
Nightmares,
I drowned in a pool,
Nightmares,
Nightmares,
Make me frown,
Nightmares,
I had one about a clown.

Jacob Alexander Mogg (9)
Milton Park Primary School, Weston-Super-Mare

Unicorn

Unicorn, unicorn
How beautiful you are
How sparkly is your horn
Shining like a star.

You're so bright
Your mane twinkles in the night
You never give a fright
You're such a delight.

When you fly
You go so high
You light up the sky
As your shining trail goes by.

Ellie Marie Havard (9)
Milton Park Primary School, Weston-Super-Mare

Really Bad Teachers

Teachers are really scratchy
Teachers are rude
Teachers are mean
Teachers are noisy.

Teachers are rude
Teachers are what?
Teachers are rude.

Oooooooo... OK

So I should never talk
To teachers and never ever
In your life, OK yeah.

Laura Widzisz (9)
Milton Park Primary School, Weston-Super-Mare

Dave The Unicorn

Dave, you are so pretty
Dave, you are majestic
Your horn, it glows in the night
Your tail, bright pink
Your hooves are full of might.

I look up to the sky
And I see one night
You riding rainbows
No one knows
When I will see
That
Light again.

Reuben Harding-Blake (8)
Milton Park Primary School, Weston-Super-Mare

Elf Onto Me!

E lf on the shelf is with me
L ook over and see
F elt tip is everywhere!

O h my goodness!
N aughty elf
T aking food from the fridge
O ff the shelf.

M oving around sneakily
E lf onto me.

Alyssa Edwards (9)
Milton Park Primary School, Weston-Super-Mare

String Dance

String dance, sing and dance
If you prance you can dance,
It is fun to have someone to dance
You can sing
You can dance
You can shake those hips and shake your pants
It is not fun to fall so string dance home
How many times can you string dance?
Ten times a day.

Aston White (9)
Milton Park Primary School, Weston-Super-Mare

Gymnastics

Do gymnastics because it's fun
Wear a sparkly leotard and your hair in a bun
Show every split to get YouTube hits
But make sure you don't get sweaty armpits
Tuck and tumble
Cartwheel and aerial
Handstand and backflip
Do all of these, you will soon need a kip.

Kayleigh Turnbull (8)
Milton Park Primary School, Weston-Super-Mare

The Right Goes Wrong

My name is Callum and I like to misbehave,
I was told by my mum not to enter this cave,
Me being me, I didn't want to listen,
As I entered the cave, I heard loud hissing,
I call out to my brother, Owen,
And the wind was howling and blowing,
When we went in, coming out was a wild boar,
Being chased by a baby dragon giving off a roar,
We've got a shed made of metal and chrome,
Owen, my brother, said, 'Let's take the dragon home.'
Me being me said, 'Yeah, but Mummy will go mad,'
'Who cares we like to be bad.'
As we're walking through our hometown,
This clown says, 'I'll buy your dragon,' with a frown
We got to our shed and snuck the dragon in,
Once back outside, we locked it with a safety pin,
Me and Owen went guiltily to our rooms,
All of a sudden, we heard a mighty boom,
Soldiers were screaming all over the place,
Me and my brother were shouting, 'What have we
done?'
Mummy didn't know and she had the only gun

Whilst the mother dragon had torn apart our garden shed
And with the horrible sight of seeing how the soldiers bled
Afterwards the mother took her baby away,
Me and Owen were so glad they didn't stay
The moral of my poem is not to misbehave
And listen to my mum, and not to enter the cave.

Callum Cairns (9)
Oasis Academy New Oak, Hengrove

Houses And Homes

I
Live
In a house
And have always
Lived in a house. But a
House is different to a home.
A home is the place where you have
Lived for a while and it's special to
You, a house is just somewhere you like
To live but don't appreciate it. My
Home is special to me because it is the
Place I am growing up. It is the place I
Bring my friends home and the place I rest
My head at night. My home is special and the
Walls are full of memories. When we moved here
Two years ago, I wasn't happy since I have lived in my
Last house for a decade. I will not move again until
I move out into my own house.

Chelsea Ince (9)
Oasis Academy New Oak, Hengrove

Flying High In The Sky

F lying high in the opal-blue sky with the clouds as
  fluffy as a pillow.
L ovely birds sing their sweet melody in the rise of the
  sun
Y oung and free, it's so lovely to be free and me.
I 'm on my own, just me and the clouds drifting on
  the horizon
N obody bothers me up in the sky while I fly really
  high
G oing high is for naturals like me and the birds in the
  opal-blue sky.

Flying high in the opal, sparkly sky is lots of fun
But when I come back down I always have fun
On the ground with my friends, sometimes you
Have to bring your flying skills down.

Courtney Kizza (9)
Oasis Academy New Oak, Hengrove

Underwater Adventure!

There was a guy named Tak,
he was having a nice time underwater.
He swam lots and lots to the bad octopus,
this octopus had stolen the precious fork that Tak
needs!
Then, Tak went to the bad octopus,
then he was given a stick,
Tak had to hit the octopus until his legs dropped the
fork!
Tak finally chopped the octopus' hand
and Tak's fork fell down so he grabbed it
and went back!
Then, Tak swam up and his ship was there,
then Tak gave the fork to the boss
and then they all went back to the island of Outpost!

Hamza Sorgucu (10)
Oasis Academy New Oak, Hengrove

Unicorns

U nderneath the hater, we all know they have a secret but you know I know too

N o one believes that unicorns are real but those that believe good things will happen to them

I nner beauty like those beautiful mythical creatures

C an I have one Mummy, all parents' nightmare is to say no so maybe when you are older

O ver and over the rainbow which you know unicorns do

R egret that you put on that show

N ever ever again

S atisfying, you know what I am on about.

Ava Bendall (10)

Oasis Academy New Oak, Hengrove

Apocalypse

A ncient warriors hunting mankind

P eople suffering from lethal blows

O rca whales swimming from total destruction

C ourageous farmers fighting for their lives

A nd outsiders try to forge weapons from the deadly battlefield

L ethal swords clash against hoes, spades and axes

Y et the outsiders are getting nowhere far

P erhaps they need some help?

S uperior gladiators help the farmers

E ventually the farmers win the savage war.

Thomas Culverhouse (10)

Oasis Academy New Oak, Hengrove

The Forgotten Pirate

When I sit on the beach, what I see is a ship sailing
towards me
I stand up and look and see a hook
Then I notice it's a pirate
Then the old wooden ship crashes against the shore
A treasure chest spills out with gold and more
What happens next is such a surprise
The treasure chest crashes onto the sand
And right there in front of my eyes, two huge
Sacks of treasure fall into my hands.

Liam Ferris (10)
Oasis Academy New Oak, Hengrove

Darkness

I'm all alone
In a pitch-black place
Nothing is around
I'm confused, I don't know what's happening
My hands are shaking in fear as I step forward
It's like there's nothing around or beyond
There's just darkness
No glimpses of light
Being alone doesn't feel nice
My body falls to the ground.

Then I woke up, it must have been a dream.

Kian Gwilliam (10)
Oasis Academy New Oak, Hengrove

Flying High

Fly little birdy, fly,
Spread your wings,
You are so high,
Above the clouds,
Beyond the trees,
High above the mounds.

Past the haunted caves,
In the dark, gloomy forest
Past the hard-working maids
Back in the nest
Well done little birdy,
Well done.

Megan Paige Williams (10)
Oasis Academy New Oak, Hengrove

Unicorns

U nicorns are useful and happy like you, rare to find

N ice and magical

I ndependent and free

C ute as a pony

O h, I wish I could see

R avishing species

N oble and divine

S mall, soft and cuddly, oh I wish it was mine!

Laya-Aria Gharyal (10)

Oasis Academy New Oak, Hengrove

Summer

Sun shining
Birds tweeting
Barbecue cooking
The wind whistling
I can smell the freshly cut flowers
Bees buzzing
We all shout,
'Water fight!'
Hooray for
Summer.

Charlotte Elizabeth Collins (10)
Oasis Academy New Oak, Hengrove

Midnight

M idnight, midnight, the stars sparkle in the sky

I magination overwhelms my eyes

D ancing in the sky, the moon was brighter than a firefly

N ot a single soul in sight

I n-between the clouds above, shone a mysterious green light

G hastly galleons rode upon the sea-like clouds

H aving a nightmare, I opened my eyes

T he first thing I saw was my mum saying, 'Bad... nightmare?'

Malakai Parsons (10)

Shakespeare Primary School, Honicknowle

Confidence

I saw something glistening in the moon-like sky
Big, round and gold
Drifting fast
Amazed and anxious
Flash of lightning, very frightening
Magic powers here we come!
Full with super confident powers
I achieved amazing things
Super-duper mathematician, super-duper driver and
best of all confidence within myself,
Another flash of lightning appeared
And I woke up to thunder and lightning!

Harry Marshall Hoskin (9)
Shakespeare Primary School, Honicknowle

When You Play Football

Football is my passion, you hear the crowd roar
On the pitch, you get a stitch when you play football
On the wing, you ping it in when you play football
Win or lose, you cannot choose when you play football
Score a goal, celebrate with your mate when you play football
Win the league, you feel fatigue, when you play football.

James Michael Hacker (10)
Shakespeare Primary School, Honicknowle

Dreams

D inosaur, dinosaur, where are you?
R oaming the land, I don't have a clue
E veryone hiding out of sight
A rghhhhh, you've given me a fright
M aybe you're real, maybe you're in my head
S leeping soundly in my bed.

Tyler Reid (10)
Shakespeare Primary School, Honicknowle

A Lego World!

I went to bed two nights ago
And woke up in a world of Lego
Later, I started walking to school
And it was really nice and cool
Roads, cars, trees, even rocks
Were all made of Lego blocks
And that was my dream!

Radu Stefan Munteanu (10)
Shakespeare Primary School, Honicknowle

Winston

I've got a dog called Winston
He is a black Staffordshire bull terrier
He's thirteen years old
I love him a lot
He has an unstable leg
But me and my family love him a lot.

Lewis Bennett (10)
Shakespeare Primary School, Honicknowle

The Clowns

C areless old clowns
L ow and big frowns
O ver all the rides
W ow but my brother sighs
N ow we say goodbye.

Kelisa Moate (10)
Shakespeare Primary School, Honicknowle

The Bullying Nightmare...

Bullying can make you feel sad
Even though you haven't done anything bad
Words that are meant to hurt,
I will wipe away like dirt,
Being left out of the game,
I feel it's rather lame,
It's time to rise above,
And fly like a dove.
Tick-tock, it's seven o'clock
No more time to mock
A new day and a new school,
Where I have been made to feel cool.
As my nightmare slowly floats away,
And becomes a happy dream to be remembered
I have to wake ready to start a school day.

India Darburn (11)
Stoke Fleming Community Primary School, Stoke Fleming

Anything

I can do anything in my dreams,
Be twenty foot tall,
Be Donald Trump and build a wall.
I could even kick a ball,
Roll in the mud,
Live in a hole I just dug,
Drink from the jug.
If I want I could be a bug,
Or sleep on a rug,
If I was taller, I could be a footballer,
Be a cat,
Eat a rat,
Be a dog,
Live in a bog,
Win all the races,
Eat strawberry laces.
I could desire man's red fire,
I could be small,
Or be a precious jewel.
But the best of all is to be me.

Alfie Rogers (9)
Stoke Fleming Community Primary School, Stoke Fleming

The Fright Of My Life!

F or my dream tonight, I could see,

R avenous monsters looking hungry,

I looked into their deadly eyes,

G leaming they were, what a surprise,

H ow did they become my biggest fear?

T hey never met me, never came near,

E pic-looking creatures they were

N ever did I reach out to touch their fur,

I wanted an amazing dream,

N o, I wanted a dream with strawberries and cream,

G ourmet doughnuts, maybe, they make a good team.

Rosie Dorothy Coombes Allen (11)
Stoke Fleming Community Primary School, Stoke Fleming

The Enchanted Forest

Running wild at night, walking through the forest,
Looking at all the flashing lights.

Weird and mysterious eyes looking at me,
Through the corner of my mind,
The dark is so scary and I'm not wanting to look
behind.

The dog whimpers and howls screaming
Through the night's darkness
Following us and our shadows that are walking far
behind us.

Walking over the cracked bridge
Getting closer and closer to the rise of the sunlight.

Iona McGhee (11)
Stoke Fleming Community Primary School, Stoke Fleming

Dreaming

D ancing polar bears through the night
R aging rapids in my mind as I turn off the light
E ating burgers bigger than me
A rghhhh, this really is a mystery!
M ischievous monkeys, I feel like screaming
I t can't be, I must be dreaming
N ever to wake up again, I'm pretty sure
G oing to sleep is not that bad anymore!

Frankie Baker (11)

Stoke Fleming Community Primary School, Stoke Fleming

Murky Woods

Misty, cold and dark
Still, quiet and scary.

Coloured eyes
Staring at us
From every which way
Scaring me even more.

The trees are antique
They look as if they're about to fall
They are lifeless.

It's mystical, magical and mysterious
I feel the shivers coming
I'm scared, petrified and spooked.

Ethan Prettyjohns (10)
Stoke Fleming Community Primary School, Stoke Fleming

Bonfire Night

I stayed in this year
But all I could hear
Was the popping of the rockets locking
Ready to fire in the air.

The fireworks were glowing
Like the bright stars at night
Everyone was excited
To look at the beautiful patterns.

Kieran Wells (11)
Stoke Fleming Community Primary School, Stoke Fleming

The Jaguar

Camouflaged against the jungle scene,
The jaguar starts to give chase,
I run into the darkness and crouch,
Hiding,
Trying to block out his evil face.

He slinks after me, following my scent,
I know it's now too late,
He's nearing my hiding place,
Only a miracle can change my fate.

He's now ten feet away,
Narrowed yellow eyes like fire,
It really doesn't look like
Soon he's going to tire.

I can hardly breathe now
He's inches from my head,
But when I open my eyes,
I'm safely in my bed.

No jaguars loom around me
No pitch-black jungle scene

Then suddenly I realised,
It was just a dream!

Or was it?

Lydia Shearman (9)
Weston All Saints Primary School, Weston

How To Become A Superhero

I had a really weird dream at night,
In which I saw an eerie light.

What was making the green glow?
Hang on, it was me, oh no!

I raced to a hospital,
They jabbed a rod up my nostril.

They proclaimed how well I was faring,
I was not good for my voice was deafening!

Then I screamed and shouted, 'Oh my!'
For now it seemed, I could fly!

I was now a super girl!
I zoomed around in a whirl.

When I was flying by,
No one would have to cry.

Then I woke up and the dream was gone,
How sad, it didn't last long!

Wait, why is my lamp glowing green?
Hey it's me, but this isn't a dream!

Rhiannon Williams (9)
Weston All Saints Primary School, Weston

The Nightmare

Once I had a horrid dream
Which made me wake up with a scream.

I was all snuggled up in bed
When gruesome things fell in my head.

I imagined that I had a mug
Full of wiggly worms and slimy slugs.

I heard a crash and the mug had shattered
All of the gruesome creatures had splattered.

All of the creatures had got everywhere
And some were even in my hair.

The next thing I knew I had woken
And the mug on my bedside was broken.

And a suspicious snail
Slid across my wall.

Olive Matilda Hosker (9)
Weston All Saints Primary School, Weston

Imagine Flying

I n the night sky, the blowing breeze when I open my window, the air against

M y face like opening a fridge, seeing glowing under my bed, looking

A t it carefully, sniffing it, smelling like strawberries, touching it now it came out

G loomy and felt a tingle down my spine but I was just fine

I started flying peacefully out my window passing Big Ben

N ot scary as the clock ticked away, seeing the cars drive by, morning now I'm

E ating breakfast with the flying pixie dust in my pocket like a bird in the sky.

Jaylen G-S (9)
Weston All Saints Primary School, Weston

Sausage Dream

I can't see, where could I be?
I'm stuck in a sausage, help me!
I can't see anyone, where could they be?
Something's hurting me, wait it feels sausagey!
The only thing to do is to eat my way out.
But I'll become as fat as a big Brussels sprout!

I can see the light with every bite
I'm out! I wonder what that dream was about?

Daniel Lawrence (9)
Weston All Saints Primary School, Weston

Jungle Dream

Tropical birds swooping through the leaves,
With frogs croaking in the trees.

I feel as if I am floating in a stream
I walk through a tropical jungle
The sun beam sparkling through the canopy.

Monkeys swing on the beams
Forming from the trees.

Falling waterfalls making tropical pools
On the forest floor.

Jack C (8)
Weston All Saints Primary School, Weston

Unicorn

Unicorns are in my dream
Unicorns are really clean
Unicorns are happy as can be
Unicorns are just like me
Unicorns are the best
Unicorns sleep in a nest
Unicorns like to eat
Unicorns have smelly feet
Unicorns have lots of friends
Unicorns are into trends
Unicorns live in a palace
Unicorns will visit Paris.

Annabelle Hicks (9)
Weston All Saints Primary School, Weston

Have You Ever Seen A Clumsy Clown?

Bouncing up and down, all around
Honk, honk on its nose,
Cheeks red as a rose,
Big feet and bigger toes
Colourful clothes
Like the rainbow's rows
Clumsy clown never gets a frown
He always gets a smile
Because people never need to fear a tear.

William Michael H (9)
Weston All Saints Primary School, Weston

Alicorns

A licorns are astonishing
L ike treble clefs with wings
I see one in my dreams,
C omposing songs for kids
O r drawing in silence
R ainbows and seas
N ow and then they come to me
S oaring on the breeze.

Sara Gabriela Stoica (9)
Weston All Saints Primary School, Weston

Believe

I got told, dreams were fake
But if you believed before you wake
And if you try with all your strength
Then your dreams may become reality
In a short length
Unicorns, dragons, I got told they're not real
But I closed my eyes and it started to reveal
I believed I said inside my head
And then I saw a unicorn in my bed
I looked at it, I saw it was dead
So I followed my heart and then looked again
It was singing and dancing in the rain
So if you believe and try your best
You could make dreams come true and show the rest
Life is too short, dreams end too soon
But if you believe and trust me too
Maybe one day, your dreams will show too.

Andrew Dyer (10)
Yeo Valley Primary School, Barnstaple

Raindrop

A
Drop
Of rain is
Like a sudden
Knock on the door
Unexpected, yet often
Welcome with a smile, it
Can brighten your day or ruin
Your plans. It can make you laugh
Or make you sad, whether the raindrop
Is moving fast or slow, or big or
Small, it always gets everyone's
Attention. A raindrop contains many secrets
It is a bubble of anticipation and
Surprise. It cleanses the Earth,
It feeds the flowers and fills the holes
The raindrop is never silent, it bangs
On the roof, spatters on the window
Or splashes into a puddle.

Lily Rose Morton (9)
Yeo Valley Primary School, Barnstaple

The Dance-Off Against Bullies

Every day, I go to school
Cuts and bruises
You try to make me look a fool,
You never even gave me a chance,
What kept me going was my love of dance.

I jump, leap and twist
The wind runs through my hair
And you may even look and stare, but I don't care
I love to dance, this may be my only chance.

Standing on the stage,
Lights shining bright,
I take a deep breath, all my dreams come true
But for some silly reason, I can't help but feel
Sorry for horrible old you.

Keila Beales-Neill (9)
Yeo Valley Primary School, Barnstaple

I'm A Robot (A Real Dream When I Was Eight)

Ding, ding, ding!
The alarm rings
There's somebody doing bad things here
Come the top cops with a *crash!*
And a swing
The robot man smashes in
The cops were in shock
Out there was work to do
So with laser eyes, the robber will fly
With a *bang*, the robber flew
With another *ping*, the jewellery breaks free
We are all safe
We are all OK, the robber is gone
Hip hip hooray!

Leo Luxton (11)
Yeo Valley Primary School, Barnstaple

Once Upon A Dream

Once upon a dream
I was a dancer
I was the best prancer
Not a great tap dancer.

Once upon a dream,
Fairies danced with me,
Beneath the blossom tree,
Getting lost in your dreams.

Once upon a dream,
I got lost easy,
With only the daisies,
To help me through my grief.

Once upon a dream,
Everything crashed down
Evil came to haunt me,
This was not meant to be.

Ella Westwood (10)
Yeo Valley Primary School, Barnstaple

Pirates At Sea

Yo ho ho and a bottle of rum,
Pirates like it in their tum.
When we're out at sea, we're wild and free
A pirate's life is the one to be
Aboard their ship is the place to be upon the sea.

Liam Leslie (10)
Yeo Valley Primary School, Barnstaple

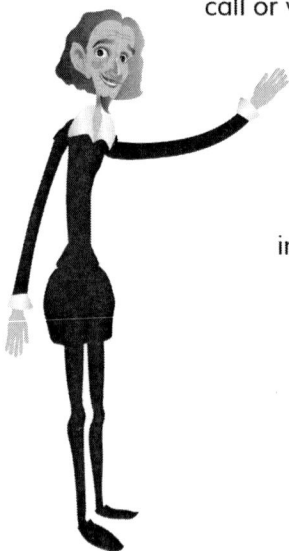